First Facts®

FACT FILES

MONEY

What You Need to Know

by JILL SHERMAN

CAPSTONE PRESS
a capstone imprint

First Facts are published by Capstone Press,
1710 Roe Crest Drive, North Mankato, Minnesota 56003
www.mycapstone.com

Library of Congress Cataloging-in-Publication Data
Library of Congress Cataloging-in-Publication data is available on the Library of Congress website.
ISBN 978-1-5157-8120-2 (library binding)
ISBN 978-1-5157-8128-8 (paperback)
ISBN 978-1-5157-8134-9 (eBook PDF)

Editorial Credits
Mandy Robbins, editor; Jenny Bergstrom, designer; Kelly Garvin, media researcher; Laura Manthe, production specialist

Photo Credits
Dreamstime/Alain Lacroix, 17; Shutterstock: 06photo, 13, Africa Studio, 15, alejandro dans neergaard, cover (bottom right), Ambient Ideas, backcover, Carolyn Franks, 4, Casper1774 Studio, 12, Cheryl Savan, 21, leungchopan, 24, Maxsol, 11, Mega Pixel, cover (top left), Monkey Business Images, 8, MPanchenko, 6, nafterphoto, 7, NAN728, 18, Neirfy, cover (top right), Olexander Zahozhyy, 9, Olleg, 22, Rawpixel.com, 16, 20, Robyn Mackenzie, cover (bottom left), 1, Rocketclips, Inc, 19, Rrraum, 5, Ryan DeBerardinis, 3

Artistic elements: Shutterstock: Happy Art, Mr. Creative, Treter

Printed in China.
010295F17

Table of Contents

What Is Money?.........................4

Money in the World.....................6

Making Money...........................8

Setting Prices.........................10

Spending Money........................12

Credit.................................14

Saving Money..........................16

Grow Your Money.......................18

Paperless Money.......................20

Glossary..............................22

Read More.............................23

Internet Sites........................23

Critical Thinking Questions...........24

Index.................................24

What Is Money?

People use money to trade for **goods** and services. Money can be broken into **units**. For example, a dollar bill can be broken into four quarters.

Many items have been used as money. In the past, people used beads, cocoa beans, and shells. Today most money is made of paper or metal.

goods—things that can be bought or sold
unit—a single person, thing, or group that is part of a larger group or whole

Money in the World

Most countries have their own money. It is their *currency*. In the United States, people use the dollar. The U.S. dollar has value everywhere. But to spend money in other countries, it must be *exchanged* for their currency.

currency—the type of money a country uses
exchange—to trade one country's money for another

6

Making Money

All people need money to buy the things they need and want. One way to get money is to have a job. Your company pays you to do work.

People can also make money by selling goods. They make a **profit** by selling goods and services for more than they cost to buy.

profit—the money that a business makes after expenses have been paid

HOW MUCH DID YOU MAKE?

**SOLD
44 GLASSES**
AT $0.25 PER GLASS
44 X 0.25 = $11.00

$11

MINUS

TOTAL
EXPENSES

$6

EQUALS

PROFIT

$5

SUPPLIES	MONEY SPENT
(capital)	(expenses)
Lemonade	$3.50
50 plastic cups	$1.50
Ice	$1.00
Pitcher	free (borrowed Mom's)
	total expenses=$6.00

Setting Prices

When setting a price for goods or services, think about **supply** and **demand**. Imagine you are selling iced tea. It's a cool day. Few people want it. Your demand is low. Your price should be low. Now imagine it's a hot day. You are the only person selling a cool drink. You can set your price higher.

supply—an amount of something that is available for use
demand—the desire to have something

PRICE OF
ICED TEA

Supply

Demand

QUANTITY
OF ICED TEA

Spending Money

Money is used to pay for needs and wants. Needs, such as groceries and housing costs, should be paid first. Wants, such as video games, can be bought with what is left.

Setting a **budget** helps people balance needs and wants. A budget helps you compare how much money you make with how much you spend.

budget—a plan for spending and saving money

Credit

Sometimes people don't have enough money. They can still buy what they need on credit. Credit is when someone buys an item now and pays for it later. They also pay **interest**. Many people use credit cards. Each month, they pay at least part of their **bill**. Eventually the whole bill must be paid, including interest.

FACT

In the United States, only adults can get credit cards. In most cases, a person must be 21 to have one.

interest—fees charged to borrow money
bill—a written record telling how much money needs to be paid

14

1

Cardholder pays for goods or services from the store.

Cardholder

Store

3

Credit Card Company bills Cardholder.

2

Store send the information to the Credit Card Company.

Credit Card Company

Saving Money

Do you want to save money to buy something later? You may want to put your money in a bank. The bank will keep your money safe. When you give your money to a bank, you are letting them borrow it. In return, the bank pays you interest.

Savings account

Enter

sign up now for more privileges

1 PEOPLE GIVE MONEY TO THE BANK.

$100

5 INTEREST!

$105

2 PEOPLE BORROW MONEY FROM THE BANK TO BUY THINGS, THEN PAY INTEREST.

$110

$105

4 THE REST IS PUT BACK.

BANK

3 THE BANKERS TAKE SOME OF THE INTEREST.

$5

Grow Your Money

Some people **invest** their money. Companies raise money by selling shares called **stocks**. Owning a share makes a person part owner of the company. When the company makes money, so do shareholders. If the company does poorly, shareholders lose money.

invest—to give or lend money to a company
stock—the value of a company, divided into shares when sold to investors

Paperless Money

Today money is often passed back and forth without any paper or coins ever changing hands. Most stores accept credit cards. People buy things and pay bills **online**. At some places, people can even access their bank accounts using their phones. One day, we may stop using paper money and coins entirely.

online—connected to or available from the Internet

Glossary

bill (BIL)—a written record telling how much money needs to be paid

budget (BUH-juht)—a plan for spending and saving money

currency (KUHR-uhn-see)—the type of money a country uses

demand (di-MAND)—the desire to have something

exchange (iks-CHAYNJ)—to trade one country's money for another

goods (GUDZ)—things that can be bought or sold

interest (IN-trist)—the cost of borrowing money

invest (in-VEST)—to give or lend money to a company

online (on-LINE)—connected to or available from the Internet

profit (PROF-it)—the money that a business makes after expenses have been paid

stock (STOK)—the value of a company divided into shares when sold to investors

supply (suh-PLY)—an amount of something that is available for use

unit (YOO-nit)—a single person, thing, or group that is part of a larger group or whole

Read More

Furgang, Kathy. *Everything Money.* National Geographic Kids. New York: National Geographic, 2013.

Jenkins, Martin. *The History of Money: From Bartering to Banking.* Somerville, Mass.: Candlewick, 2014.

Reina, Mary. *Learn About Money.* Money and You. North Mankato, Minn.: Capstone Publishing, 2015.

Internet Sites

Use FactHound find Internet sites related to this book.

Visit *www.facthound.com*

Just type in 9781515781202

Super-cool stuff!

Check out projects, games and lots more at
www.capstonekids.com

Critical Thinking Questions

1. How would it affect your iced tea sales if someone else was selling iced tea on your street?

2. What is the benefit of putting your money in a bank?

3. Name two ways to get money.

Index

banks, 16, 20

bills, 14, 20

budgets, 12

credit, 14, 20

demand, 10

dollars, 4, 6

euros, 6

interest, 14, 16

investing, 18

needs, 8, 12, 14

prices, 10

profits, 8

saving money, 16

supply, 10

wants, 8, 12